INSPIRED

MY THOUGHTS REVEALED

SYLVANUS BANINI

Order this book online at www.trafford.com
or email orders@trafford.com

Most Trafford titles are also available at major online book retailers.

Printed in the United States of America.

ISBN: 978-1-4669-3344-6 (sc)
ISBN: 978-1-4669-3345-3 (e)

Trafford rev. 06/12/2012

 www.trafford.com

North America & international
toll-free: 1 888 232 4444 (USA & Canada)
phone: 250 383 6864 ♦ fax: 812 355 4082

CONTENTS

I give thanks to God for making this book a reality, also to my better half for encouraging and supporting me; to my beautiful daughter whose birth Inspired me, not forgetting everyone that believed in me especially an uncle whose published poem also Inspired me.

I AM NOT A POET

but I write my thoughts
it may sound good
some time it becomes noise
but this is what I am blessed with
the nonsense in my heart
which I could gossip it
do I care if you dare to understand
if you read it well
you will know me
because I live in the lines
the sweet
the bitter
and
the sour
I am not a poet

CONTRAST, WAR, REALITY

A gun that kills
A gun that saves
The wrath of the wicked
Is the cry of the innocent
Advantage of the stronger
Is the pain of the sufferer
People destroy for joy
And People destroy to avenge
A blood that stains yet blood that cleanses
A death may be a blessing
A living may be a hell
Every say is good but bad when one benefit
Lone say is bad some good
Save a child and you thus preserve a nation
Love a woman, peace at home
Strength of the man security assured

Pain is politics but politics is joy
Diplomacy is a fabrication to a selfish gain
Yet it is the legitimate path to united race thus, generating a
common good
A united race; a stable world
Preserve nature is to
Prolong mortality.

INNER WORLD

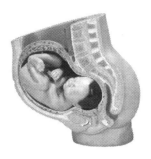

A world indeed yet not aware of
A planet inhibited by one
A world you dwell for long in controlled
Yet dwell for short in isolation
Another mouth eats while it digest in
Another's stomach
Even though mobile yet stationed
You can be seen and be felt but cannot be seen
Surviving depends on another yet an individual
With an own soul
The most cared for but cannot be touched
Yet at sight, you insight happiness
You exist by the laws yet
You know not your existence
So dark in the world;
Still find your way out with your head
And thus your innocent cry
Makes us smile
Your joyful arrival is a pain in between and the whole
Because the inner world has never held more than nine;
A peculiar world indeed

SUPREME

He sees so vast;
so was told by the last
these greatness are life's author
thus, deem it suitable to be invincible till later.
Some kill for; yet was told He died for
They fear the wrath of the unknown
So powerful that he rule alone
Deadly are his wrath yet they love with all
Your greatest bad and good; to him is small
They seek yet when they find they hide
The wise question, but they chide.
These brave never contest
Because the supreme never detest
Any power that refuses are dethrone
And thus must condone.

MEMORIES OF A BOY

They made me enjoy part of the future in the past,
Come I did not, yet enjoyed till its last
Then, an abomination
But now a private celebration
It is a battle that yields not death
The pleasure of a sensual pressure rendered me deaf

A beautiful past yielding an ugly future
Was physical, yet I sought for the remedies in literature
So sweet an act; that rewards
Yet it's consequences are backwards
Was in the suppose care of a loner
Enjoyed as an elder

In a midst of darkness my eyes open even in tender
A fellow in a sensual crime; yet a victim in
An embraced agenda
At the peak of this strenuous journey
Able and the qualified ceases
Prematurely in harmony
Even as she enjoys my youth, thus, nullifies
The thought of a future agony

My vigorous panting was no threat
Thus the genesis of my physique to her was a flirt
Flash backs makes me wish I was
I knew not then, now the pleasure is the cause
An initiation in to a world not yet accepted
Yet in smiles I enter to my rejection
Although my prompt attempts was a seduction
There goes unconcern worries
And thus, my bitter sweet memories

I WILL LET YOU GO

A warrior as I am
I fear not what comes my way
I have been to the extreme
Obstacles are discarded like insects
My commands are obeyed like a tyrant
Never had I given up
Yet I begged for your love
I will let you go

My pain was your joy
My depreciates was your appreciates
My poverty was to your riches
My dislike and insecurity was to your strength
My love was your lust
For you my best was not good enough
I will let you go

I strive for your delightful moans at night
Yet my partial absence was my nonexistence
Smiles shown to my presence
But your eyes reveal otherwise
I yearn to love; your love I fear
I will let you go

The sum of my innocent love
Equals the sum of your steered hate
I have conquered, yet I can't conquer
I love you to hate me
The warmth of your embraced chills my soul yet I cherish
The ambition of your hidden romance, thus, I fear
I will let you go

RED BLOOD

Black or white red blood
Muslim, Christian needs a life
Right to live was so bad
Living the life yet striving hard
Look beyond anger and you will
See that love motivates
Experience hate and you will dare death
They seek and hear not your pain
Speak their wish and their effort is in vain
West, East, South or North one world
Try to save and you are a tyrant
Perish while trying and
You are a hero
A slave or a master
Red blood

DIVIDED NATIONS

We came together to unite
In the climax of suspicion
Years not long passed
An enemy smiled death
Impending doom raised a bond
Yet we agree on condition

Like the hunter
Fearless as the lion
In a combined strength
With the dance of death
The stronger now the weaker
Subdued was a beast
A present hate reveals
A hidden love

Under a roof of unity
We kill with civility
Against death in uniform
A vision of coexistence
Yet we sold the love
In search for mortality
Destruction evolves
Thus divided we stand.

THE POET

Words of wisdom are read
But after they exist in the air
After they exist in names
After they exist on stone walls

Read the writings
Yet cannot read the readings
Like a painter;
Words are irrational,
Yet when cease to exist;
A literal hero
Same language but hear it new

The truth uncovered
Yet hidden in words
Genuinely written insane
But words that bring fame

CHILD SOLDIER

They cry for help
Yet we dance to politics
Their effort becomes our success
We watch them die
Their innocence stained with ignorance
Thus see dead as sleep
They who inherit our achievements
We kill with our ambitions
Though man cherish power
We leave none to obey
We give to them our sins
To kill and flirt with death
The only reward we give to the innocent
The mornings in them
Replaces our evenings
They pull a silent trigger
And fear the deadly sound
Soon there will be no future
When the child become a messenger of death the soldier

A CRY WAS HEARD

But in the midst of joy,
A bitter sweet moment,
In love; embraced in skin,
A bond never to be broken evolves,
In pain, in tears, reality of the moment smiles,
Yet my nie nie nie was a sign of life,
She stroke my bare, but original body,
Rub me with care against her nude,
There I knew not the feelings of excitement, yet I knew love,
Little was my eyes, yet I saw deep;
In her heart was the best for my existence,
I love you,
For you gave life,
For being that vessel,
From thee a cry was heard,
From thee a poet was begat.

HEAR MY VOICE

On the other side of existence
She wished for my voice
Thus I speak but silent sounds echoes on paper
And it says I sound like a man
I sound like a boy
I am a man
I desire a heart
I sound like you read
I sound like I am
Read me and you hear me
My voice echoes in sweetness
It calls your name, like a queen
Like a princess
Like a lady you are
It sounds like I look
Like I behave
Like I touch
Like I do
Like I like

I WANT TO KNOW

Do you want to know?
Do you want to hear?
Do you even want to see?
No baby I don't want to know the pain I caused you,
I don't want to know the discomfort I caused you,
Not the emotional stress I caused you darling.
But sweetheart, I want to see the smiles I bring to thee,
My queen I want to know the pleasure I caused you,
I want to hear the joy of my presence, my lady.
Baby if you can forget, you will remember never to forget;
The sweetness of my love,
The other side of my desire,
The good of my bad,
The dream that I dream
And when you do
It makes me feel like him again,
My queen it makes me love you like a princess,
It makes the future like present
Thus, love becomes lovely like the word love,
Perhaps I want to know.

CALL IT GOOD

Well I thought you will like to read.
Have fun reading
It scares yet it is sweet
When you fear it is good
When you fear not it was great
It is you; it is I it is us
But it is red
It is essential
Sometimes it divides
But it should unite

WHAT IS LOVE

LOVE IS BITTER, LOVE IS SWEET,
MAN IGNORES THE DARK SIDE
THUS EMBRACE THE LIGHT OF A TICKING FEELING,
WHEN THE OTHER SIDE OF OUR DEFINED LOVE PASS;
IT TAKES IT SHARE OF THE CONSTITUTION OF LOVE,
THEN WE STUPIDLY CONFUSED, SEPARATE
TO ALLOW AGAIN; THE SWEETNESS OF A BAD
DEFINITION;PATHOS NOT LOVE, FORGIVE ME IF MY
LOVE IS DIFFERENT, I LOVE YOU

A HIDDEN POWER

I was born in the darkness,
Shaped in the shadows,
I am the beauty of a bad silhouette,
So special that I evolved from across the seas, deserts, the far dark
west,
I am that use to tone all others to reveal a hidden beauty,
I am from the worst that the best must go to make news,
But I am that can never hate but can only love,
I am the dirty that is beautiful
I am of the second; the third
where my sweat and products makes the first,
I am the superpower.

A QUEEN I TREAT

A queen I treat though you despise
Tis you that sees not
Thus call a beauty a beast
Deep down lies life passage
There in greed you seek love
Up within a core a love we share
A smile you seek a frown you reject
That you reject a smile I seek.

DAY DREAMING

Together in the silhouette of light,
A cloudy night but no rains,
The moon watches in awe of moments as my hands traces the
contours of a beauty,
Encompass by nature; the logo of GODs creation consume our
infatuated moans,
There your lips enlightened my heart with desire,
And behold, like a man I grab to hold but wait
The voice of my boss wakes me from lover's world.

THIS POEM

I write this poem in my medieval self
I write this poem in front of my Victorian balcony
In the spirit when love is seldom reciprocated I write this
Like a Sicilian guard waiting and ready to pounce to defend
Thus, is my patience and love
In the environment of mistress and servant, a slave seeks love
in a madam
Like the morning dew yielding an impaired vision; a beautiful
profile I see,
My infatuations like a historian confidence; not sure of the truth
Question me beyond desire and I will flirt like a bordello girl
The tales of "Lady high heel" hunted my youth,
Now the ecstasy of femininity searches' to devour my chastity
A lone in bed I wrestle to free me from the spells of bachelor's
culture
Yet the comfort of the bed inculcate in me the sweetness of the
"first sin"
In the Garden of Eden
Like the youth David, I confide in the likes of Jonathan yet I fear
The wrath of his father
Lust differ from love yet without the lust of love your love will cease
to last
Out of ignorance a lay person will believe that Salahadin defeated
Napoleon, Hannibal conquered Jerusalem, Socrates defended O.J
Simpson, and Timbuktu is the capital of the British Empire, odyssey
was a disciple and Idi Amin was a protestant priest,

Such is my unlettered love,
Silent night holy night, but within the grips of darkness
fornication a fashion
And silence reveals the sobs of tainted affection
In the midst of segregated words the beauty of silence revealed
in this poem.

WHAT IF I'M A CRIMINAL

I see you enjoy my good name
I see you embrace my identity
You clad yourself with my past
You stand tall from my sweat
Though you knew not me, my success thus, your success
What you inherit you sweat not for
So what if I'm a criminal

You ask me not yet you consume
I stop by and was told you beat me to it
Covert I and all have I add
I am known for what I can
Yet you regard less of the sweet that yield sour
Impostor of the horrible enjoy naught to last
The dream you sabotage I yield not to thee
So what if I'm a criminal

When you thought I see not
When you felt you deserve better
When ye knew you will not be caught
You ignored the pain, the torture of the mind
You wanted it yet you feared to account for
Even when you know you were hoaxing
So what if I'm a criminal

When you know I deserve it
When you know I strive for
When you know I yearn for
Yet you covert; you snatched
So what if I'm a criminal

BEYOND THE SMILES

look at my face and its all smiles
and then you desire to smile back
you then wish me good
even though you failed to see beyond the smiles
you deduce not that I'm human
thus, the absolute you seek I have not
the weakness you feared me to have perhaps have I
like my kind, a smile may be a pretends
like many of my kind greed, power, fear and desire seeks
Beyond beyond

I AM GROWING

The mirror revealed various exits of aging contour lines
Under the sinking weary eyes
At the wash of yesterday a new life sprung forth to battle The
resistance of today
Years past when the early birds music reminds of yesterday's Childs
play, thus, it lure me to lust today's little adventure
Tomorrow comes screaming of a deviated vision
Now I wake to the noise of a busy alarm in a far away land
Only to be reminded of a child long dream at the tick of time
And the screams of the watchful machine "riches are yet to be made"
Now the brain of age ponder over tomorrow
When the ignorance of yesterday was the only adventure
Once blend with smooth and youth
Now blessed with rough and tough
Thus my sustained marriage with aging pain
Paves way to the eternal nothing

LUST WORLD

Lust you may seek my desire
But my heart you will find not
Thus the protection of love have I
Though the strength of desire supersede my resistance
Yet the wrath of morality creates a barrier of affection
Knowingly have I dared you
Willingly not seeking thee in the lands far beyond my reach
Thus I wake to hide your presence
Yet in the lands of the honeymooners a host
In the chamber of procreation you may dwell
For thy eminence in limited love
I will dare you shew when the light dims out
Hence in aw of exultation
The moans escaping my sheets shall bid thee farewell
Abolishing your presence from the corridors of emotions for
In my heart a love presides over the union
And slowly the bond of friendship with lust ceases
Thus the absence of ritual fidelity
Deeply felt in the heart
Of unchaste virgins

SO SHE SMILED

It was like pain yet it did not hurt
I dread a heart attack when I gasped for air
And thus she smiled
Her teeth was so white
It almost robbed me off my sight
So I dared to speak the words I hear them not
For what I hear I spake never before
Many a beauty have I laid a bachelors sight
Yet the sight of her compels me to glorify the maker
Then it hit me, did I just say "yes I do"
Ha-ha I hope she did not hear
Again she smiled
O "thou" little cupid will you strike her
For this wall of troy enslaves dearest love
Then I heard a voice oops it is proceeding forth from within
Telling me to go for it, damn it
Then she smiled
Oh my God the smile so beautiful;
I was wondering
Is she the daughter of Helen
All the charms of a man have I

Yet she falls not
In her eyes I look as the gaze draws her nearer
Oh my what a sight
The preservation of virginity surrounds every dance of walk
Like afar of she smiled
Drenched in love dripping a sweat of mental intercourse
The sparks of the sun scorch me not
And when she stood and stared; I felt it
I wanted to see
I wanted to jump
I wanted to smile
I wanted to cry
I wanted to run
I wanted to sit
I wanted to dance
I wanted to hug
I wanted to kiss
I wanted to taste
I wanted to touch
And
I wanted it all
And then it came to me, this time it was a song
"Is this love, is this love is this love that am feeling"
So she smiled.

THE LETTER

I thought I should email you
Then I realized if I should
Words hidden in the chamber of love
I may not be able to type
So I write on a medium whose sacrifices yields a space
Only fit to reveal feelings difficult to describe
Then in writing I sleep
Leaving the hands to speak what the hearts feels
Then I dreamt
You appeared
In silence you talked with your stare
Why do you love me
Now hear the heart talk
The hands move not, yet the pen writes

In my greed have I imagine living without you
But a second away and I yearn for the smell of your presence
Then I knew I love you because I do
It is that when I desire separation
I tend to regret immediately
It is that which makes a vowed man
share tears like a child
O yes have I loved before
Yet with you I am
A prince
The lover
The handsome
A celebrity
Precious
A jewel
A hero
Accepted and
Sought after
In fact you make me feel at best
Relaxed when I am at rest
Even so darling
You remind me of
A beauty in a tale
A flower that I came across
A river that quench my thirst
The air that sustain my life
Dearest, in my softy quest to seek love
You are the feeling that I desire to possess
A song that I wish to know how to sing

A world that I yearn to dwell in
Oops a sound, a sound
The fire alarm
Smoke, smoke, smoke every where
Did I sleep Ha ha ha
Again thinking of thee put me to sleep
O my tis your thought that burn my food
Yet for love I care less
For in dream I can only smell your sweetness
I now I awake to write
The LETTER

A BEAUTIFUL PREY

In my capacity to devour a fearful
Yet a beautiful prey
I have stumble across sweetness
That ceases not with it effect in my heart
Though the strength, the energy I possess
I have not the vigor to resist the inner weakness
Such is the beauty of a warrior
Like a hunter I dance my victory dance
Yet the victor who bleeds in excitement
Is my prey
The sweet I devour now paves way
For the sour hidden in beauty
Then my eye opens to see not
A way out of this infatuated field of teeth
Grinding singles

Then reality becomes a puzzle only to be
Solved to be a step ahead of authority
Thus eighteen of the Lords birth celebration
Shall pass by
Before I sing to freedom, veiling me from
The venom of the next prey
And yet the yoke of pressure
Insight a hidden pleasure
For thus I hunt with care to exhume lust treasure
For the spells of her flirts
I stand no chance, though I come prepared as a hunter
Again a curse of remittances I incur
Yet the angels of my blood will I love
To benefit my beautiful prey

I WANT TO BE LIKE THEM

I want to be like them,
Feel strong, loved, admired like the star
I will not mind the extra care like a brand new car
Yet use by the right heart gentile but firm
I hate to be asked twice because I am from there
I am ready to let go the sweet bad desire
Such an incongruous bench mark, enough to retire
O what a shame, I yearn their likes but I feared to dare
The look of a man my face enunciate
Yet the elements of narcissism refuse a friendly smile
I wonder why she taste me sweet, when the core I taste a bile
So to be like them will I dissociate from their ignorance
So have I come to learn the ghost of bigotry
For the dark of a dance reveals my story
From whence comest thou
Thou speak not when I smile
You let me go in shame
Though I speak your language
O what a world
You seek a friend but they smile hatred
Am I right to be selfish
Am I right to hate
Can I just be accepted
I am of the other skin
Though I see but the blood flow red
Do you feel the pain
Any way I want to be like them.

I WANT TO BE A CANDIDATE

I want to be a candidate
Yet I fear to be the winner
For those whose course I fight fails to appreciate
Beguiled by the spices of many thoughts I am branded the sinner
I was once hailed; the child of unity
Now in the dungeon of emotions I question my integrity

I want to be a candidate
Forgive my innocence if I tend to indoctrinate
My heart saddens when I dance to the power of secrecy
Though have I dined with elements of civil intimacy
I want to be on the lips of the young as a natured revolution
Come to naught in a senseless evolution

I want to be a candidate
Striving my conscience yielding to the norms of the aggregate
Thus, bearing the encumbrance of your discussion
I will execute my aspiration with precision
Thus, when I cease to be, I will live within education
Remember, like the many "great" before me; I am the thought
writer
Many of my generation refuse I hither

Because have I become pregnant with words
I have been abandoned in grips of a spoken identity
Captured in the war of thoughts
I have become a prisoner of a voice
Hidden to all ears
It comes to me when I seek not

THE BOND

never been so high
with my peers, I have cease to ask why
for the course we procreate, we can't say bye
thus, for the love of brotherhood we reject a lie
I can promise you this, our success look to the sky
for if we fail at first, we will grow when we try
and in the sky our philosophy thus, fly
seeking a heart of faith to tie
the feeling of I and I oh my
for the bond of love till we die

NATURAL RHYTHM

It begins with pain, a mother's cry at labor
Ends with pain, a relatives cry at burial
In the hour of matrimony smiles, smiling to the rhythm of love
Such is the hour of procreation; you thrust out your likeness in
smiles
And when fortune fines you;
Whence comest thy love ones you know not
But let the cruelty of poverty declare its allegiance to you
And a curse of loneliness is the measure of your personality
Infidelity the rhythm of the unfaithful
And when lifted to the realm of visions, you despise the beautiful
In this structured revelation
Wisdom now branded the voice of the past
Thus, the tales of many great thinkers mythically celebrated
I am a pair of eyes, dancing to the rhythm of my bearer's emotion
Thus, the bearer is not exempt from covetousness
Like the stories were told

Survival was begat in the master's garden
But the beauty of this rhythm is such
Before the battle of nine months
Before the first cry of a life
There was a constant rhythm

. . . .

WATCH OUT

I am not a friend
Neither am I the enemy
I don't care if you don't care
I prefer to be left a lone
What a pity, should you cross my path
I don't know you
I know not if you know me
I like my self
I will climb high to preserve the self
I will smile when it is funny
But you will not like the smile if you are not what you are
Because I will not hesitate to be in a state of nature
What you feel keep to your self
For your woes are the least of my cares
I know you think I'm bad
But yey I'm sad
Yes that's what you want
Better stay out of my way
And let the lone heart lay
For such tears will not sway . . . .

A LINE FROM THE DREAM

It started with a dance
The region around what mine eyes saw I cared less
Every fold of a man in me, stupidly glued at her beauty
And all I see was the curves from a woman
Swinging to a every noise of the sound
That steals her from mine greed
Thus, the anger was for all the lousy looks of predators
I wanted her all for mine eyes
But her innocence drives an angel to the four corners of the
discotheque
Yet I still gaze with delight, with greed
And with the vigor of a warrior
Felt like strangling any soul that will steal a glance at a beauty
I know not

As she draws nearer, mine feet moves mine thought
So drench in the pheromone of her womanhood
I trail every step with an ecstasy of a mild smile of a bad man
Only desiring to be that scantily clad attire
Along the bumpy terrains of her sweaty body
And solely enjoying the warmth of this "hottie"
Then I stretch forth to grab her beautifully created waist
But before any part of me can feel this sweetie
The clock rings . . . it's time to wake
For mine daily bread will have to be earn
Wish I can dream you again
Mine dear creation

DEEP THOUGHTS

Regression and repression
Emulate depression and their impression
Welcome to the conscious kingdom
I am a warrior in the mental warfare
A written revolution to end the anti-love regime
I am not wicked I am what I am, a mirror
I speak the people's voice in the mind politics
I am the language that you hate to speak
Want to know the truth listen to the voice that throbs in the heart

NEVER TO SEEK YOU AWAY FROM YOU

I thought I could do without you
Never realized the beauty of seeing with both two
Thus, I stroll in search of peace away from home
As I drive among them, yet I felt their comfort cage me a lone
Beyond the horizon yet visible in the thick of darkness
These vehicles appeared without the brightness of two
The first, second and the third, and my
I thought how clumsy the look of luxury,
Even as it approaches without the perfection of both light
Then I see how beauty is covered in darkness without its perfect
match
Finally it dawn on me how stupid, I seek peace away from peace
For you my love is my peace
Thus, home I come in the waiting arms of my sweet, my heart
Never to feel alone, never to seek you away from you

WILL YOU BE MY VAL

And when I descend on to thy lips like in the dreams
And when you yearn to wake and feel the breath of desire
Then will I plead with thee to lie still
And to bequeath to me thy charming beauty
Beneath the warmth of mine sensual covers
Whilst my soul roams every mountain and valley along thy Exposed
beauty of yet another perfect creation
Of HIM that the books talk of
In search of the passage of life
A natural quest of every man
Thus every thrust of excitement
That follows the moans of acceptance dear
Will I ask thee a question that will only yield the joy of saying
"Aye aye" in my chamber;
Will you be my VAL

YET TO NO AVAIL

And we kill so hard
Though the lust of puberty has cease not to pass
And in the midst of the soldiers adventure,
A nobility of the highest revered accorded to the corpses of the young
recruits
Thus pain engulfed in the emotion,
Identifies an unaccomplished journey in the weary wrinkled eye of
the family
While an infant stare at the weeping rituals dedicated at a fathers
sleeping body,
Yet to no avail,
The infants' subsequent cry for love, for future unanswered
The father he never had, he cries to
Whose promised future prematurely discontinued
To the covetous ideals of a modern system

A CHILD HE MAY NEVER SEE

Tis the last lust within
The little chambers of delusional ecstasy,
When he danced to the rhythm scarcely known
To the world of the young in the land of the singles,
Thus, he drenched the drip of life into
The exciting cries beneath his sweaty figure,
Which favor the dominant pressure of the man
In the act of carnal knowledge,
Then when morning comes
Then when life retraces glory
Then when man must survive
Yet again the vengeance of yester-life failure,
A soldier does a soldier's way
Farewell without a hint of fear or love to his mistress,
Off to the battle front to defend the greed of the masters of the
universe,
Thus, soaked in tears,
She cries to yet again
The likely fate of today's young soldier,
A child he may never see,
Conceived in the shadows of the night before the morning comes.

THE MARK OF THE HOUR

Delightfully in pain
When the only hate I love
Strangles me in the art of seduction
Thus, I pounce to render the joy
Of a man's savagery
Likewise a whisper yet so loud in my ears
The voices of the dark, illuminating
The fate of excitement in an ungodly hour
Far beyond the horizon of orgasm
Deep in the reign of ecstasy
I reject the laws of chastity
Thus, I am marked with the gift of the hour
From whence I go, I returned not a boy
Neither do I yearn to flirt with
The woes of maturity
Yet the appellations from the mark I dance to,
O what a journey
Mystify by the sweetness of its sourness.

IT WAS ALL I LONGED FOR

Across the oceans to the land of Riches,
Lays Freedom and Possibilities
Stained with the norm of my customs
Hardly can I yearn the lust of the West
Then it came with gifts, sweetened and scented with promises
Of a new birth beyond the skies
From whence the big and noisy bird will take me in its belly
Yet it was all I longed for
Away from home,
Away from custom,
Away from love,
Away from myself,
Away from this life
And away from the torture of poverty
And the tyranny of blood thirst leadership
Though a disciples of that tradition,
Yet I embrace the flirts of the new order
Oh what a world
A room have I; the comfy of my lonely bed have I not
Like the hardship soldier,
I serve the economy sixteen hours in a day
Enjoying the warmth of my abode less
Transit points have I become for the currency
In a sweet bitter affair of the new world
Yet it was all I longed for

BEFORE THE RAINS

Before the rains
The wind blows
And the harvest smells within
Tis the farmer to plant the good seeds on time
If the land stays bare
The plant life will be eroded
A downpour we seek
Yet when it overflows,
We curse from whence
It cometh with our tears
Famine in the wet season?
A good farmer thus, know
Before the rains

RESET MY HEART BEAT MY LOVE

When mine eyes caught a glimpse of you
Mine heart did skip a beat
At first I thought, I thought it was an irregular
Heart beat, then I feared,
I thought I will reveal how
Shy your beauty imposed on me,
So I ignored the feelings thinking I could dance it off,
But the instant I held you,
I knew it, like every man's prayer
HE has answered mine,
O Mather I have found mine treasure;
She who melts the very man in me out
Leaving me again like the child I once was,
How I want to love you
How I want to protect you

How I want to hold you
How I want to kiss you
How I want you so bad
And when you are out of my sight
Mine love grows even stronger
Days without you seem to me like eternity
Then I knew
You alone can mend my heart
You alone will I ever love
You alone can I ever be mine self
Dearest now I know
That heart beat I skipped was your heart I felt
It was the love we share
It was that first beat that I will never forget
Because it is that skipped beat that always reset
My love for you,
It is always there
Feeding me with your love

LOVE

The word love will often cross my mind,
My heart and then I speak it
The only standard definition that I find within my soul
Can only be traced to you my love,
Thus, Tis your face
Brightening with the sweet smiles
Tis your lips; I am so hypnotized by the beauty
To which the lovely rhythm of your words
As you speak love to me dearest,
Tis your contour; every inch of your womanhood
Is preserved in aura of love
Sweetheart, you have struck a chord in
My heart and it sings out a melody of love full of
The light and happiness for our future,
Together we become a team that defies all of
The impediments of love and life trials
Above all your desire to seek HE the Creator first
Have assured me of the peace
I am bound to have in your love.

SLEEPLESS NIGHT

I bid thee sweet dreams
Only to lay and stare at your stunning beauty
You lay motionless bare to the skin; gone to the dreams
Whilst I watch every inch of your innocence glowing to my
desire
Thus, I am rapturously delighted in a mental foreplay
As I fondle my way down every region of your femininity in lust
Yet bound by love, I respect your willingness to not yield to my
flirts tonight
Whilst you lay scantily clad in a loincloth; revealing and
inviting
Unaware of the spell that you have sensually cast on me even in
your sleep
Sleepless night have I, as I stare in the dark
Romancing to my imagination and yearning over the silhouette
of a beautiful lover.

THE MARK OF THE HOUR

Delightfully in pain
When the only hate I love
Strangles me in the art of seduction
Thus, I pounce to render the joy
Of man's savagery
Like a whisper yet so loud in my ears
The voices of the dark, illuminating
The fate of excitement in an ungodly hour
Far beyond the horizon of orgasm
Deep in the reign of ecstasy
I reject the laws of chastity
Thus I am marked with the gift of the hour
From whence I go, I returned not a boy
Neither do I yearn to flirt with
The woes of maturity
Yet the appellations from the mark I dance to
O what a journey
Mystify by the sweetness of its sourness
I'm marked by the hour

THE LOVE STORY

The broken heart once love a heart
But lack of understanding made love hurt
Lovers in this time call it a quit
But my time seems not to fit
It saddens me to see my best halve
To leave a perfect bond, put together by the good old man
In search of a supposed true one
Who will eventually have none
To offer a sweet and a lonely love
This once flew across my heart like a dove
And will never feel the sweet pain
Of the lover ready to tame

O what a flower that I had always wished for
May find it sensual likeness by my door
As I get nearer to the barrier of nakedness
I sense the everlasting feelings of oneness
At last there is joy in my home
Like how the pope storms Rome
Our bed is delightfully wet
And the daring preparation of procreation is set
The sweet good night songs and bye byes are said with kisses
Such is how celestial love in a romantic room at night
But I wake; the same old love story
Regretful of my choices feeling all sorry
Once more I have been struck by cupid
Oh, how suddenly I feel stupid
For love washes down the path in my heart like a stream
After all it was the same old dream.

AND WE KILL SO HARD

Though the lust of puberty has cease not to pass
And in the midst of the soldiers adventure,
A nobility of the highest revered
Accorded to the corpses of the young recruits
Thus pain engulfed in emotion,
Identifies an unaccomplished journey
In the weary wrinkled eye of the family
While an infant stare at the weeping rituals
Dedicated to the fathers sleeping body
Yet to no avail,
The cry of a child
Unanswered by the lifeless body of
The father he never had
Who's promised future
Prematurely discontinued
To the covetous ideals of a modern system

A TASTE OF WAR

The cries echoed revenge
Such was the barbaric visualization of
Insecurity at the global edge
Critical at the core; among inhabitants of the east
Of a motherland
Shaped by beauty, adventure, wild and wealth
Proclaimed to be the genesis of humanity
Cultured in great traditions
Smiled over the riches of great land
Enjoyed the scenery of the wild and its beasts
Now sadly dance to death by their greed
Ooh mama Africa, I seek your revenge against the destructors
Yet I refuse to be part of the brutality of revenge killings
Death must, but by the hands of the great one
And by the spirits of the forefathers
Not through a taste of war
The people of the first, return to your roots
And let the nature of our trees be our likeness

SLEEP

When it want to come
You feel it weights wanting
To shut your windows to this world
And when it finally sets in
How you left the world is never remembered
Yet it marks of dreams can be
A mark ever or never to wanting to bear
Then your motionless body
Lays undefended from the attacks of
The blackout lord,
Yet when it comes not
You yearn for this erased period of your life
Sleep.

I AM SORRY

It begins with lovers jokes
Romance touches of the strong man
The feminine tease of the woman flirts
And the bedroom brawl of who wants it
Soon emotion sets in
From the unwelcome calls on his phone
And her superiority texting to
The jealous ears of her true friends
Soon the aura of suspicion set in
And the drama of love evolves
Full of bitter sweet affairs
Yet at the rush of his thrust
And at the joy of her ride
It was the fame of I am sorry
That set the chemistry right.

SUCH IS LIFE

When you are blessed with what you want
When you needeth it not
Yet compelled by fashion to put on the dreamers grin
A smile as sweet as the sourness of a desirable gin
Thus, the era when many yearn for happiness
To define a reward you desire not it sweetness
Yet embrace an unjustifiable means
Whilst you swallow the fingers that mortifies your pride
And walk the humble walk of the progenitor
And watch that blessing become
The dream that you fancied at yester year
Perhaps a blessing or a curse
Should propagate such doctrine as
Such is life.

NOTHING

Like the saying goes
In order to experience death
Look at sleep
The art of dying
Whilst you roam a world
Built on unconscious imaginations
Steered by accumulations of your emotions
Then you wake to joy if by your design
Or to fear and pain all by your design
For every night
Whilst you lay still and walk the vision quest
You virtually rehearse the moment of nothingness
When the lifelong peace you seek
Finds you with the aid of the still dark lord of death
And returns you no more to life and pain
You thus realize that you are not rehearsing the inevitable
But in the icy grips of the lords of nothing

THE UNITED UNION

When I become like them
I will be not like them
I will seek to destroy the peace
That they endure in their destruction
And the evil that they have embraced
In their united objectives
Thus will I seek to eradicate
Whilst I sneak in
The benefits of collaboration
Whilst I strive for knowledge, understanding
And wisdom within diverse regions
Yet I will flirt with the sentiment in our secluded devotion
To a branded religion
Where equanimity will become a pursuant
To norm in the state of nature
And in the midst of the union
Where contention among contenders
Are resolved in spite of oppositions
In The United Union
Of counteract pals.

THE JOURNEY HOME

One day I will go
And on that fearful day
Will you let the ocean deep down
Within your soul flood not
For the said moment tarry
Yet it comes in the shadow of life
Tis a journey to fulfill a promised
Cessation to the tribulation brought to by ageing
Yet tis a sanctuary for the stiffen bones of hard labor
An ambience of nothing in the thick of darkness
Where the stain on the flesh determine not
Your place among your kind
Thus tis the journey home
This evokes heartbreaking emotions
Leaving the lagoon below the window of life
Drained in salty stream
Down the countenance of the self
Yet a pilgrimage to discover the hidden truths of life

MADAME

The philosophical mind
The intellectual mind
The reserved nature
Of a noble gentlemen
With such a humble nature
In a celestial state of intent
Has been subdued
By the power and innocence
Yet ambitious beauty such as you possess

Madame
Should such a flower dwell within
The borders of my reign
How perfect my heart will find you as the queen
To rule my humble abode
And to keep my chambers hot enough
To warm away the chills suffered by lonely warriors

Madame
Whilst caged in the norm of life
The custom of culture
Yet I have been able to crack open the societal identity
To express the sweetness in your beauty
How fragrantly scented your beauty is
Bursting out of you a light of intelligence
The seducing nature of your attractive innocence
Thus keeps my driven vision alive

Madame
Your unintentional ignorance
Of my admiration
Punish my ambition
My desire
My melodious
Yet annoyed cries
Aimed at impeding your dedication to chastity
Resembling the passion Romeo had for Rosaline before Juliet
Like a warrior
I give up not to my unreciprocated lust
While romancing to the dreams at night in my chambers
That secretly
You are enjoying the weakness
That your beauty cast on me
Whilst the jealous world stare in limbo
Of the drama between I and the Madame

SMUGGLED

All the characteristics of my influence
I feel bad within
The pain I cause
The cancer
The insanity
The killings
Unnecessary hallucinations
The robberies
The premarital sex
The impaired visions
The tainted wisdom
Yet I'm greatly impressed
For
I stopped the suicidal thoughts
I caused the instant joy but short
My presence crushed away the gruesome pain
When I'm used rightly I perform wonders
Names have I been called
Even now my identity is lost
Though I was nurtured and nursed with care
Yet I'm a hardened criminal in the lands
So lonely was I that I was hidden while growing
Still hidden I perform wonders
In the eyes of those who bare my mark
Their language I speak not
Yet when I am active in them
They speak me like a mother to a child

They think they can discern my intentions
But I know they don't
Just like any of my kind
I prefer to be used right
I like to enjoy my privacy
Yet I hate to be summoned secretly
I make them rich
Wherever I go they light me up
I am the forest within the cities
I am the most traveled among my kind
Because I was smuggled

SMUGGLED.